THINK
ON TH
YOU

MARY HATHAWAY
ILLUSTRATIONS BY JULIA ROWNTREE

Some thoughts and prayers
on the birth of your child

To

Billy & Mary

From

John & Sheila McKelvey

On the occasion of

....

....

Date

....

JOY AND LAUGHTER

The Lord has filled my heart with gladness,
he has given me joy and laughter!

At last I am satisfied,
for I have found part of myself
I have always been looking for
in the tiny person
of my new-born child!

MIRACLE

Creator of all things,
watch over the sowing of love
in this young life.

Guide me through the early months of
tenderness and care,
feeling hesitant and sometimes inadequate,
while I get used to this tremendous miracle
that is my child.

Then over the years,
as the seed takes root,
help us both to grow in love and wisdom.

Grant that I may see the harvest of love
in this life
and rejoice in remembering this special time
of birth.

CREATIVE LOVE

I want to give you
a childhood of happy memories.
I want to love you creatively
so that there are many
specific happy moments
for you to remember with joy
for the rest of your life.

And I pray
that you may absorb
the creative love
surrounding you.
So that you can find joy
within yourself,
and that this may give you
the ability to make
happy memories for yourself
and others.

Already you give so much joy—
may you continue to find
and give joy always.

FIRST SMILE

From your birth
my love shone into you
and smouldered into flame.
Love was kindled in you,
lighting lamps in your eyes —
today I saw the beginning
of all your loving
in your first smile.

SHARED JOY

You are yourself, my child,
not a replica of me
or of anyone.
You will have your own ideas
of what is beautiful.

So moments of shared joy,
when gladness glows
in both of us
because some
fragment of glory
has touched our lives
at the same time,
are rare and precious,
not to be grasped at,
not to be expected,
or accepted as our right,
but to be treasured
as an unmerited gift of God.

LOVE LAUGHTER

Some laughter is good
and some is bad,
but there is pure laughter,
there is joyous laughter,
when a child laughs at the morning
brilliant with sunlight,
spontaneous and free.

And there is the laughter
that spills over from a heart
that is filled to the brim with love.

This laughter is warm, gentle and kind.
It is always joyous, pure and lovely.

May you know early in your life, my child,
this best gift of love laughter.

THE GIFT OF A CHILD

Lord, help me
in my relationship
as a parent to my child.
Help me to remember
that my child is your gift
and to thank you

even when my patience is taxed
to the uttermost!
Help me never to take this gift for granted
but to be grateful that you have
entrusted a child to my care
to bring up and love for you.

TO MY CHILD

In silence I watch
the expressions
on your face, so mobile, so alert,
soaking up each detail
of the room,
every part of you
throbbing with life
and yet gladly absorbing
the stillness,
each moment like a story
never to be retold.
Neither yesterday or tomorrow
can have these special joys.

So our love finds room
to expand in the stillness
and our knowledge of each other
grows a little more each day
in the unhurried, lamp-lit joy
of these quiet hours.

A BLESSING

May the Lord bless you
and take care of you;
May the Lord be kind and gracious to you;
May the Lord look on you with favour
and give you peace.

From the Book of Numbers, chapter 6

Children are a gift from the Lord;
they are a real blessing.

From Psalm 127

J esus said,
'Let the children come to me,
and do not stop them,
because the kingdom of God belongs to such as
these . . .'

Then he took the children in his arms,
placed his hands on each one of them,
and blessed them.

From Mark's Gospel, chapter 10

EVENING PRAYER

My child, as I look at you
in the shadows of evening,
I commit you to God
for the oncoming night.

May he enfold you
and cradle you gently—
sleep well, little one,
as you lie in his arms.

Published by
Lion Publishing plc
Icknield Way, Tring, Herts, England
ISBN 0 7459 1421 7
Albatross Books Pty Ltd
PO Box 320, Sutherland, NSW 2232, Australia
ISBN 0 86760 935 4

First edition 1988

Acknowledgments
Bible quotations are from the *Good News Bible*,
copyright 1966, 1971 and 1976 American Bible Society,
published by the Bible Societies/Collins

Printed and bound in Italy